Adaptation fr...
Rabbi Sofer Ro...

Rabbi
Akiva's
Letters

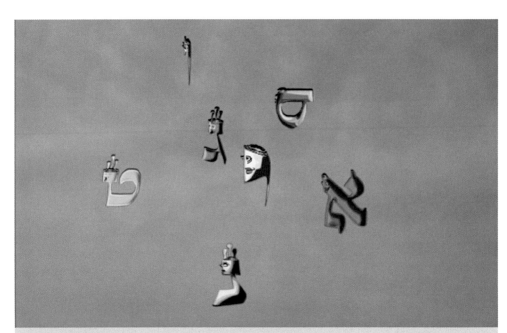

Just before the creation of the world, all of the letters gathered around all wanting to be the very first letter in the Torah and first letter in creation.

My name is Rabbi Akiva and these are the 22 letters of which the entire Torah was given to the Tribes of Israel.

First approached Tov
Master of the Universe,
may it be Your Will to begin the creation
of the whole world with me because, I begin...

תָּו   ת

TOV = 400

תּוֹרָה

Torah

תְּהִלָּה

Tehilla - Song

תְּפִלָּה

Tefilla - Prayer

תּוֹרָה צִוָּה לָנוּ מֹשֶׁה

Torah Tziva Lanu Moshe
Torah Commanded Us By Moses

As it is written, with me You will give the Torah to Israel by the hand of Moshe. I'm the highest number from all the letters pick me please to be the first.

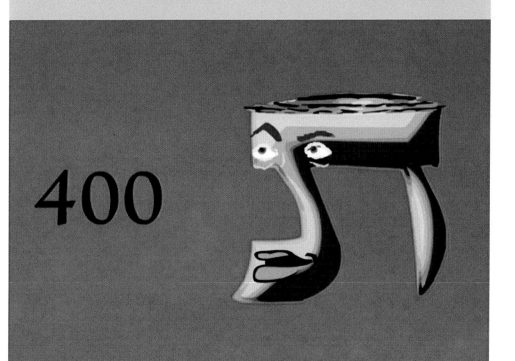

400

תְּלוּנָה

Teluna

Complaint

The Almighty answered the Tov with a flat out NO. Well, when the Good Lord said that, wouldn't you know it, Tov backed away fearfully disappointed.

שָׁלוֹם

PEACE
SHALOM

After which came up the Shinn and sat before the Holy One, Blessed be He.

300

Master of the world, may it be Your Will,
use me to begin the world that You will create
because I guard over the Shabos.

שׁוֹמֵר שַׁבָּת

Shomer Shabos
Guard Over The Sabath

עוֹשֶׂה שָׁלוֹם בִּמְרוֹמָיו

Oseh Shalom Bimromav

He Who Makes Peace in Heaven

הוּא יַעֲשֶׂה שָׁלוֹם עָלֵינוּ

Hoo Yaseh Shalom Alaynu

May He Make Peace For Us

שֶׁקֶר
Sheker
Lie

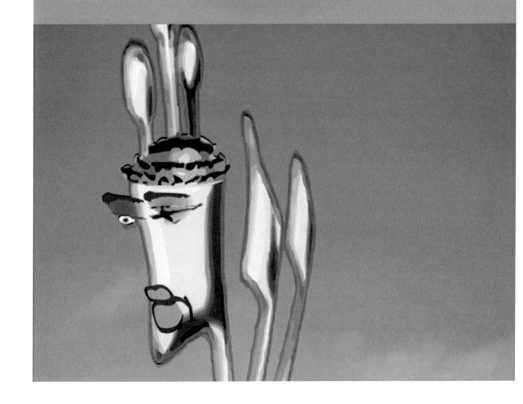

ש שִׁין

SHINN = 300

The Lord answered the Shinn with a NO because Sheker starts with a shinn and a sheker is a lie and a lie has nothing to stand on. The Shinn backed up.

ר רֵישׁ

RAISH = 200

Start with me Master of the Universe,
I begin Your name Rachum meaning Merciful One.

נָחוּם
Rachum
Merciful
רְפוּאָה
Rafua
Medicine

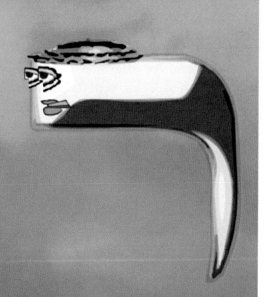

200

ראשׁ
Rosh - Head
ראשׁ הַשָּׁנָה
Rosh HaShanah
New Year
or Head of the Year

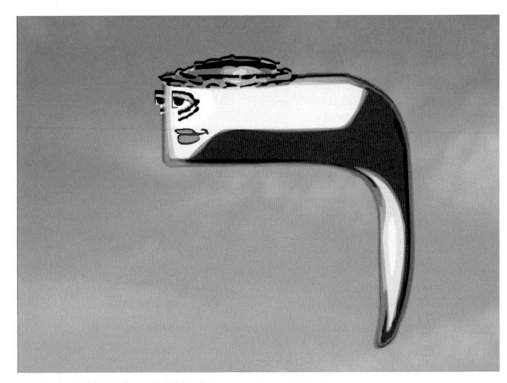

The Good Lord Answered the Raish, No.
Because starting with you will be the word wicked...
upon hearing this the Raish backed down scared.

רָשָׁע

Rasha
Wicked

Koof moves in to give it his best try. May it be Your Will to create the world starting with me because with me it is called out about Your Holiness.

ק   קוף

KOOF = 100

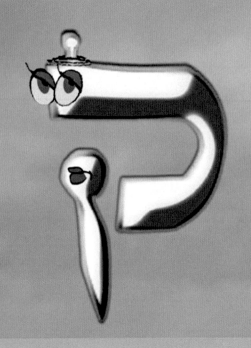

קָדוֹשׁ
Kadosh
Holy

100

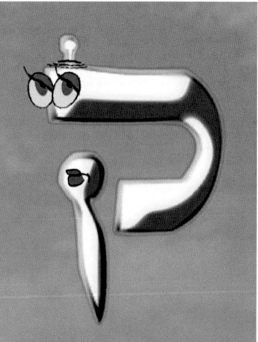

קֶרֶן

Keren
Fund

קְלָלוֹת

Klalot
Curses

The Holy One, Blessed Be He, replied to the Koof, No, from you will come into the world curses.
Upon hearing this the Koof backed away.

Tsadik sees his chance and approaches the front.

צ צַדִיק

TSADIK = 90

צַדִּיק

Tzadik
Righteous

צַדִּיק הַשֵׁם

Tzadik Hashem

Righteous is the Lord

צְדָקוֹת אוֹהֵב

Tzedakos Ohev

Righteousness He Loves

90

Start the creation of everything with me. The Holy One, Blessed Be He answers the Tsadik with a No. One at a time, the other letters keep coming up.

צֶמַח

Tsemach

Sprout Forth

צְדָקָה

Tzadaka

Charity

פ   פֵה

PAI = 80

פּוֹדֶה

Pode

Redeemer

פֵּירוֹת

Payrot

Fruit

פְּנֵי

Pnay

Face of

80

פָּרוּעַ

Parua

Wild

Out Of Control

עַיִן

Ayin   Eye

עֵינַיִים

Aynayeem Eyes

ע   עַיִן

AHYIN = 70

עוֹלָם
Olam
World

When the Ahyin heard The Holy One, Blessed Be He said no, he backed away embarassed. After that came the Samech's request before the Amighty.

עוֹז
Ohz
Grandeur

עֲבֵירָה
Avayra
sin

ס   סָמֶךְ

SAMECH = 60

סֻכָּה
Sukkah - Hut

סִימָן
Seemon - Sign

סִדּוּר
Siddur - Prayer Book

סוֹף

Sof

End

60

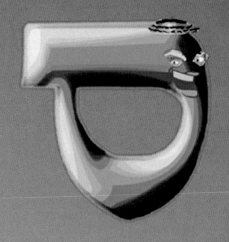

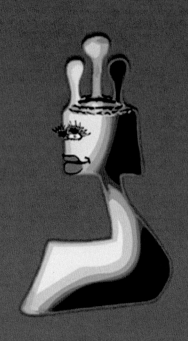

נ נון

NOON = 50

נֵר
Nair
Light

50

נְשָׁמָה
Neshama
Soul

40

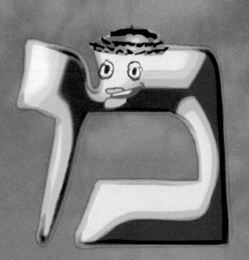

Master of the World can You create the world starting with me? For sure You agree, right?

מֶלֶךְ מַלְכֵי הַמְּלָכִים

Melech
Malchay
Hamlachim
King Of All Kings

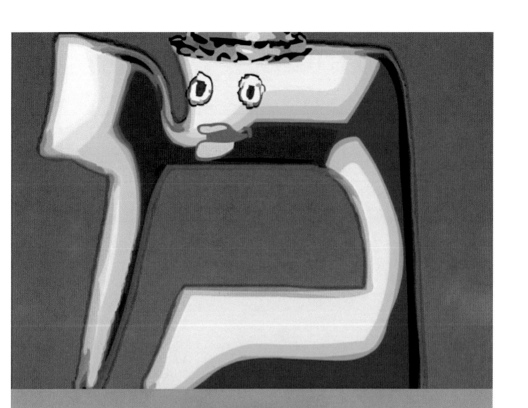

מֶלֶךְ

Melech

King

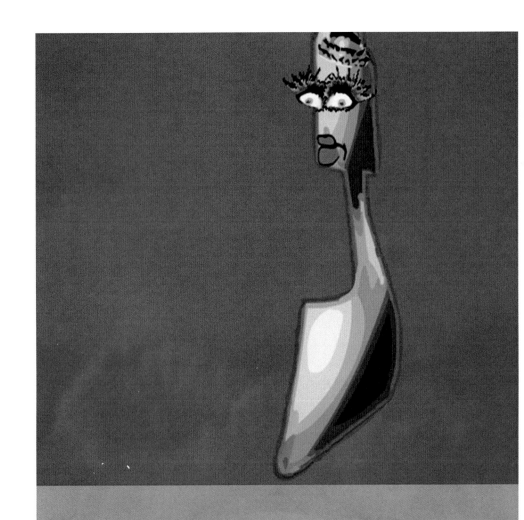

נוּדְנִיק

Nudnik
bothersome

מָלֵא
Maleh - Fill

מַיִם
Mayim - Water

מָגֵן
Magen - Shield

מֵם　　　מ

MEM = 40

מְהוּמָה
Mehuma
Confusion

The Good Lord answered the Mem, No.
Upon hearing this the Mem backed down scared.

ל לָמֶד

LAMMED = 30

לִלְמוֹד
Lilmod
To Learn
וּלְלַמֵד
LeLamed
And To Teach

All Mighty One, I am the tallest of all the letters.
When I wave my crown it is clearly seen
that Lammed is truly above all the rest.

לַמְדָן

Lamdan
Scholar

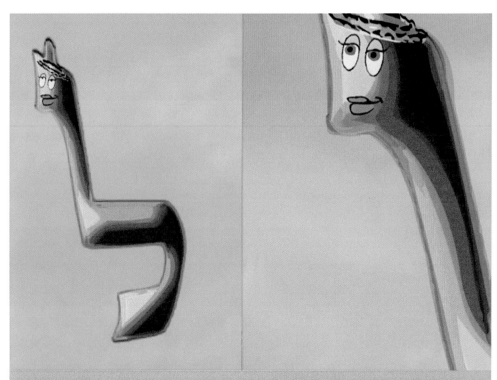

From you will come into the world the word tablets and they will be broken so I certainly can not create the world starting with you. Lammed backed away.

30

לוּחוֹת

Loochos
Tablets

Dear Lord, the Torah should certainly start with me.

כַּף כ

KAF = 20

20

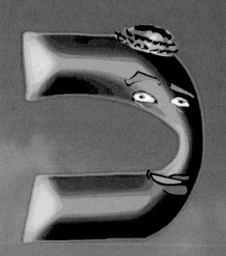

כִּסֵּא כָּבוֹד

Seat of Honor

Keesay Cavod

כֶּתֶר

Kesser
Crown

G-d Almighty answered the Kaf, No.
The Kaf backed away. Then came the Yud.

כְּלוּם

Kloom
Nothing

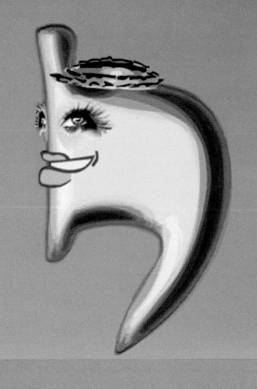

יוֹד י

YUD = 10

יוֹם

Yom

Day

יְחִי
Yechi
To Live

יְהוּדִי
Yehudi
Jewish

יַעֲנֵנוּ
Yanaynu
He Will Answer Us

10

The Good Lord Answered as well to the Yud, No.
Upon hearing this the Yud backed down scared.

יוֹם הַדִּין

Yom Hadin
Day Of Judgement

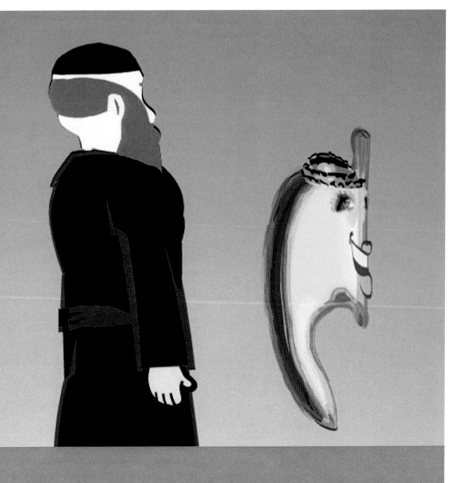

יֵצֶר הָרַע

Yetzer Harah
Evil Inclination

ט   טֵית

TESS = 9

טוֹב

Tov

Good

טָהוֹר
Tahor
Pure

חֲנֻכָּה

CHANUKAH

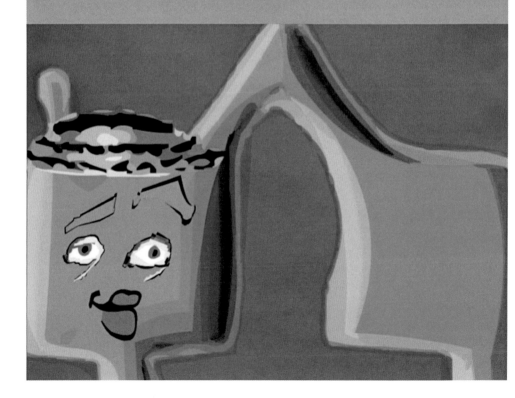

9

The Answer to Tess was No.
Then Ches came up for a try.

טַעַם
Taʿam
Taste

חַנּוּן

Chanun
Merciful

חֶסֶד

Chesed
Kindness

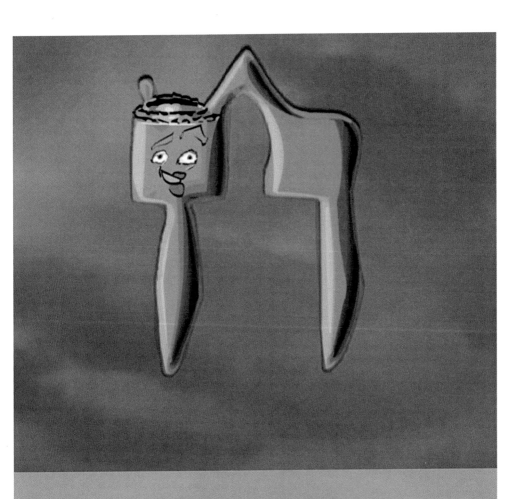

ח   חֵית

CHES = 8

8

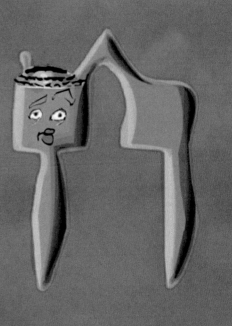

The Good Lord Answered the Ches, No.
Starting with you will be the word for sin.
Hearing this the Ches backed down scared.

חָטָא

Chaita

Sin

זְכוּת
Zechoos
Merit

Holy Master, create the world starting with Zayen.

7

זִמְרָה
Zeemra
Song

פְּסוּקֵי דְזִמְרָה
Psukay DeZimra
Verses of Song

זַיִן ז

ZAYEN = 7

זֵכֶר

Zecher
Memory

זִכְרְךָ לְדּוֹר וָדֹר

Zeechrecha
L'Dor V'Dor
Your Memory Will
Stand Forever

זְלְזוּל
Zilzool
Disrespect

The Good Lord answered the Zayen, No.
Because Zayen starts the word for disrespect.
The Zayen backed away giving the Vov a chance.

וָו֫   וֹ

VOV = 6

וְ

Ve

And

וְאַתָּה קָדוֹשׁ

Ve-Atta Kadosh

And You Are Holy

אַתָּה וְאֲנִי

Atta Ve-Anee

You And Me

וֶרֶד

Vered Rose

וַיִּקְרָא

Vayikra
And He Summoned

The Almighty, Blessed Be He, tells Vov, No.
Vov starts the middle of the Torah. How can the
middle start the beginning. Hai approaches next.

6

ה הֵא הָא

HAI = 5

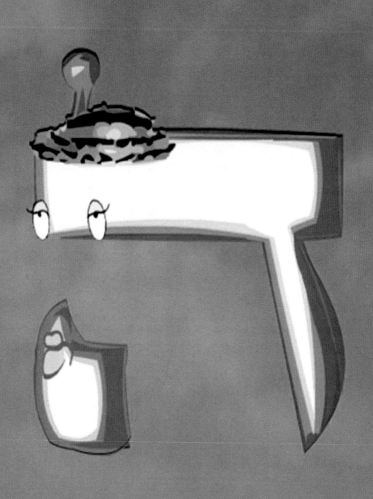

הוֹד
Hod
Beauty

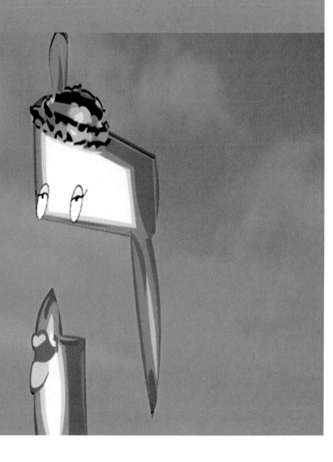

הָדָר

Hadar
Majesty

When the Almighty Creator answered the Hai, No, the Hai backed away making room for the Dalet.

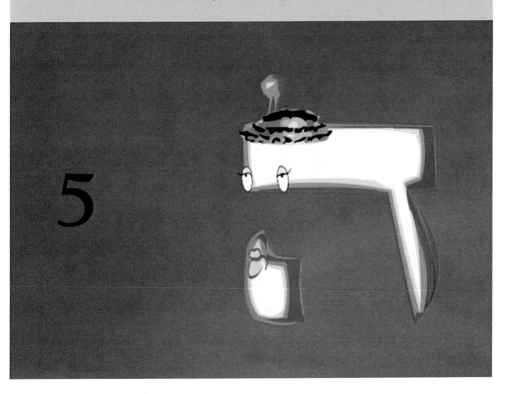

5

ד   דָּלֶת

Dalet = 4

דֶּלֶת

Delet
Door

דָּוִד הַמֶּלֶךְ

King David

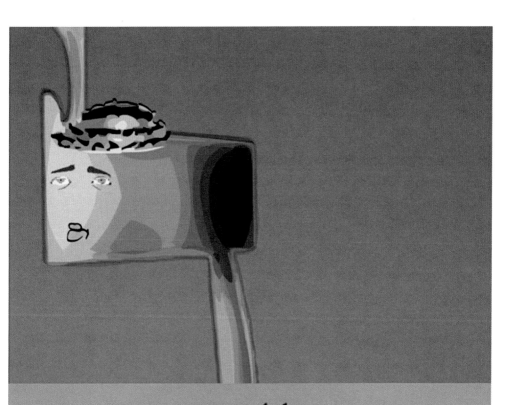

דִּין
Din
Judgement

בֵּין דִּין לְדִין
Bayn Din Le Din
From Judgement
To Judgement

4

The Good Lord answered the Dalet with a No.
The Dalet backed away giving the Gimmel a chance.

דּוֹר לְדוֹר

Dor Le Dor

Generation to Generation

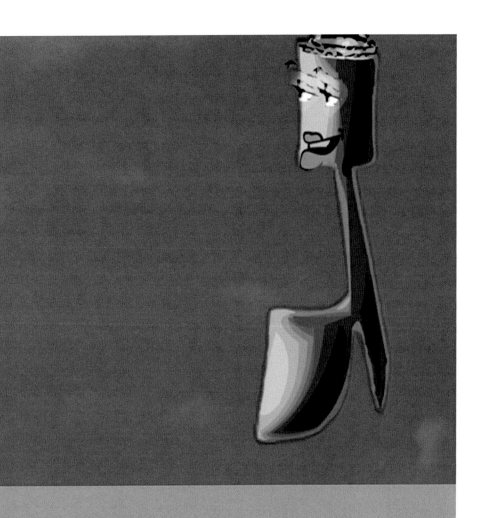

ג   גָמָל

GIMMEL = 3

גַּדְלוּת

Gadloot
Greatness

3

גְּבוּרוֹת

Gvoorot
Powerful

גוּפִי

Goofy
as in
Goof-Ball
also means
My Body

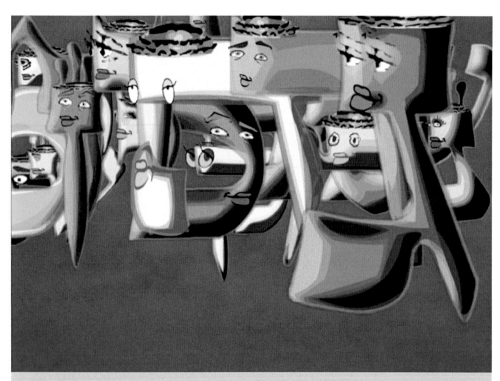

All the other letters were hiding behind one another not wanting to be first, they all backed up farther. Only Alef and Bais had not yet asked to go first.

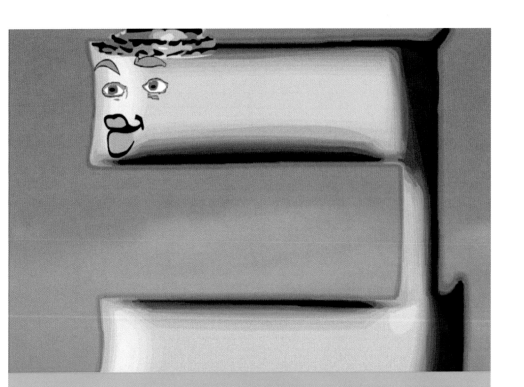

ב   בֵּית

BAIS = 2

בָּרוּךְ ה'

Baruch HaShem

Blessed Is The Lord

Blessed are Your Lord. With me the Children of
Israel bless each other sanctifying Your Holy Name.
On this G-d decided, Yes, start the Torah with Bais.

בְּרֵאשִׁית בָּרָא ה'

Braishis Barrah

In The Beggining
G-d Created

2

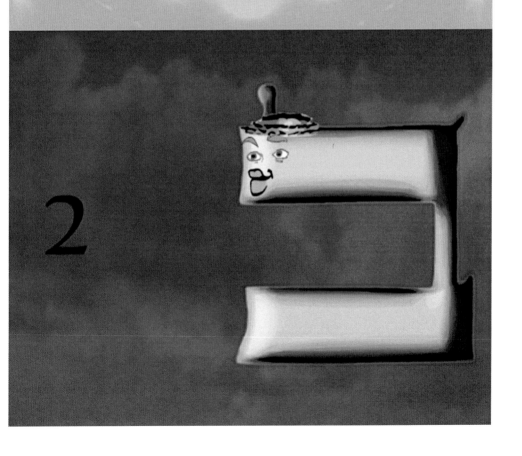

The Almighty Lord asked Alef, Alef why are you going away without asking anything from me? Master of the Universe it really doesn't matter much now anyway. I'm such an unimportant letter, the other letters all make a sound and I am silent, they are all worth more than me, Bais is 2, Dalet is 4, Kaf is 20, Koof is 100 and I am but one.

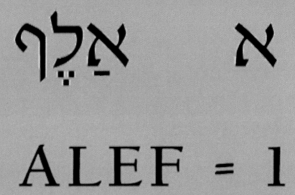

אֶלֶף   א

ALEF = 1

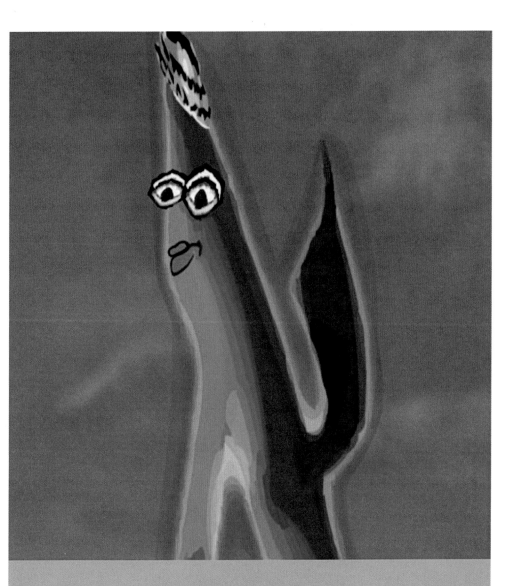

אֱמֶת
Emes
Truth
Truth Of The Torah

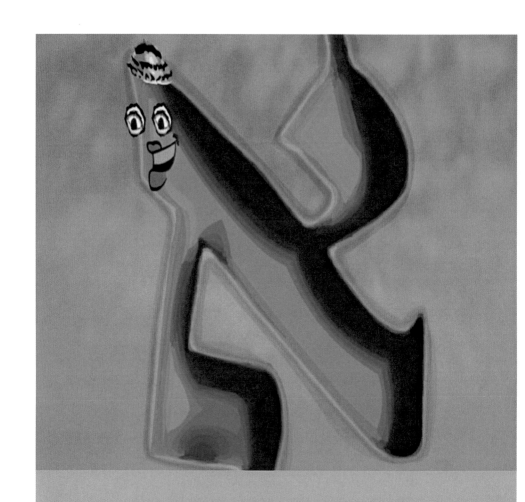

G-d is 1
Alef is 1
Torah is 1

1

Don't worry Alef you will become their leader like a king. When I give the Torah at Mount Sinai, I will begin with none other than you. Alef will be the first letter In the first of the Ten commandments.

אָנוֹכִי ה

Anochee Hashem
I Am The Lord

Alef starts the line up like a natural leader with Bais
and the other letters all finding places right behind.

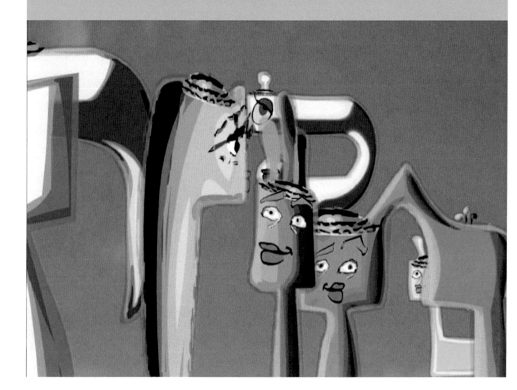

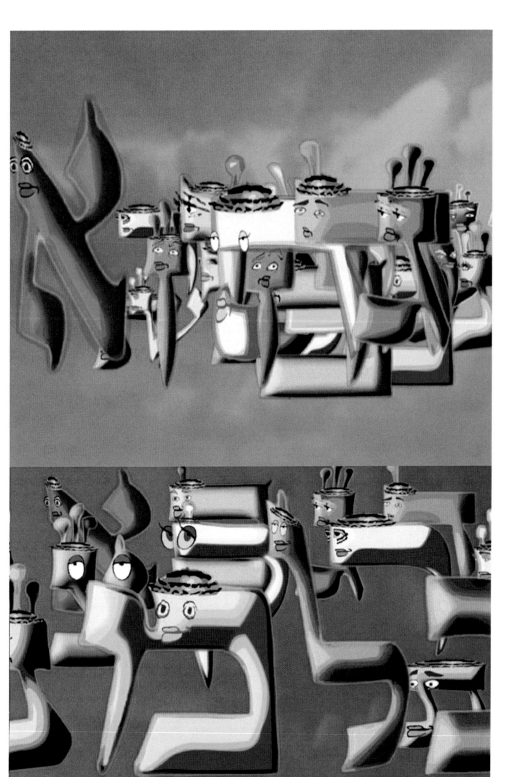

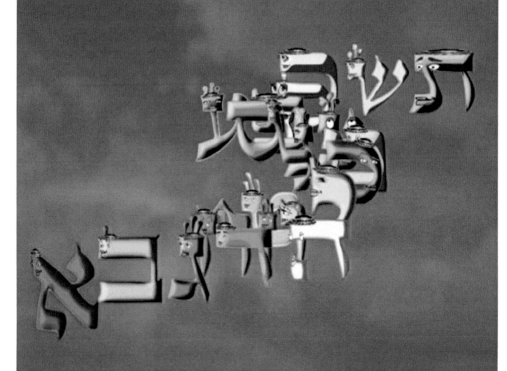

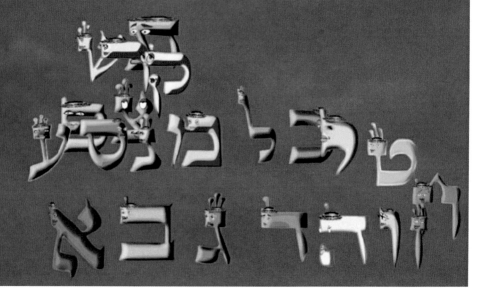

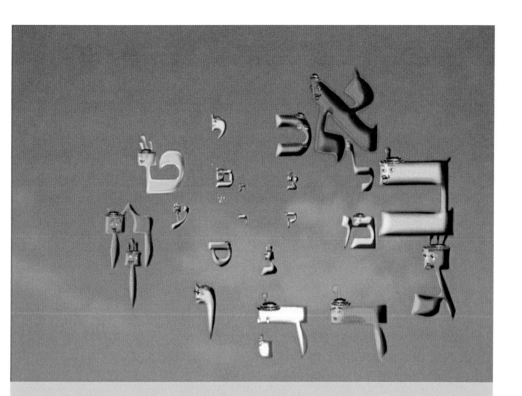

And thats how the 22 Hebrew Letters came to be ordered; Alef, Bais, Gimmel, Dalet, Hai, Vov, Zayen, Ches, Tess, Yud, Kaf, Lammed, Mem, Noon, Samech, Ahyen, Pai, Tsadik, Koof, Raish, Shinn and Tov.

סוף

Sof

End

Made in United States
Orlando, FL
25 April 2025